FRUIT

HEALTHY EATING

BY GEMMA McMULLEN

CONTENTS

Look out for the underlined words in this book, they are explained in the glossary on page 24.

© This edition was published in 2017. First published in 2016.

Book Life
King's Lynn
Norfolk PE30 4LS

ISBN:978-1-910512-40-1

All rights reserved
Printed in Malaysia

Written by:
Gemma McMullen

Edited by:
Grace Jones

Designed by:
Ian McMullen

A catalogue record for this book is available from the British Library.

WHAT IS A FRUIT?

A fruit is the part of a plant where seeds are found. Fruits are usually sweet and juicy and can be eaten <u>raw</u>.

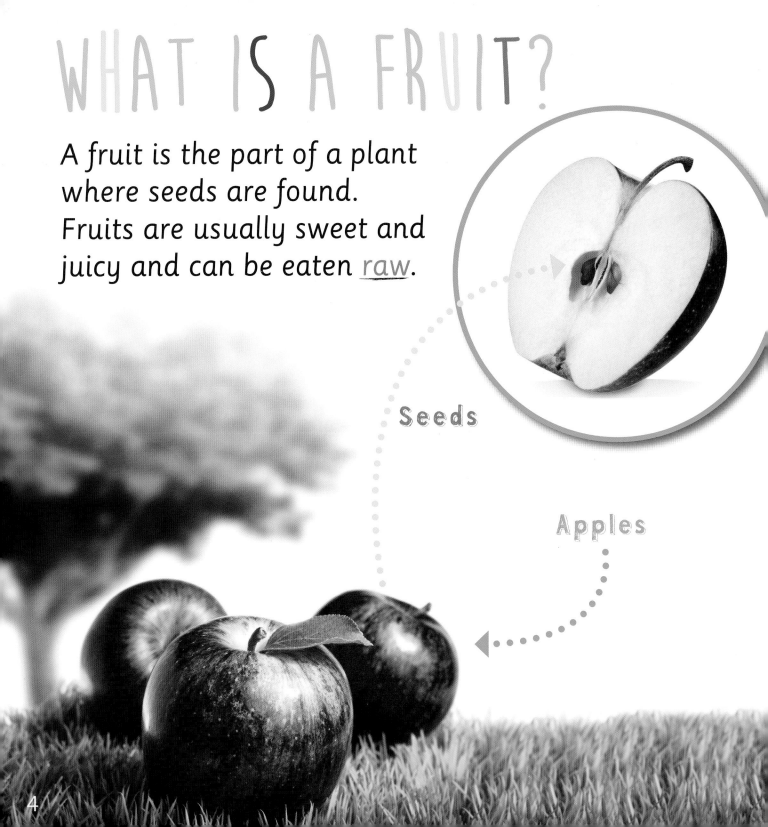

Seeds

Apples

Only plants that flower produce fruit.

Blossom from an orange tree.

The blossom grows into an orange.

FRUIT GROWS ON TREES

Some fruits grow on trees. First, the trees produce flowers and then the fruit grows. When the fruit is ripe, it falls to the ground. Some of the seeds inside the fallen fruit might grow into new trees.

Some fruits can only grow in hot <u>climates</u>, such as the coconut and the mango.

Coconut Tree

Even though its name suggests that it is a nut, the coconut is a fruit.

7

FRUIT GROWS ON BUSHES

Raspberries

Blackberries

Some fruits grow on bushes. Their sweet taste and bright colours often mean that they attract birds. The birds spread the seeds so that they might grow into new bushes.

Fruit farms grow large amounts of fruit so that it can be sold to shops and supermarkets.

Many fruit farms allow people to come and help pick their fruit in the summer.

FRUIT GROWS ON VINES

Some fruits grow on vines. Some vine plants grow upwards and some grow along the ground, such as melon plants.

Passion fruit

Grapes

Melons

The tomato is sometimes mistaken for a vegetable, but it is a fruit. Tomatoes are one of the easiest vine fruits to grow.

There are over 10 thousand varieties of tomato!

HEALTHY FRUIT

Fruit is very good for our bodies because it contains important <u>vitamins and minerals</u>.

You should try to eat fruit every day.

Check the labels on food to see how much fruit they contain.

Fruit is most healthy when it is eaten raw. Sweets and drinks containing fruit also contain a lot of sugar.

WHERE DO WE GET FRUIT FROM?

Most people buy their fruit from supermarkets or greengrocers. Fruit grown in our country is usually cheaper to buy than fruit grown in other countries.

Some people grow their own fruit in their gardens or <u>allotments</u>. If they produce a lot of fruit, they might sell it or give some to their family and friends.

Does any fruit grow in your garden?

WHICH FRUIT DO YOU LIKE BEST?

There are many different fruits that you can try. Which one do you like the best? Are there any fruits that you don't like?

Which fruit is dried to make a raisin?

Fruit can be eaten in many different ways. Some people like to eat dried fruit, such as raisins. Other people bake fruit and use it in pies and crumbles.

TROPICAL FRUITS

Tropical fruits come from countries that are warm and wet for much of the year.

They are usually very sweet and taste nice in fruit salads and smoothies.

Tropical fruits from other countries are brought over to the UK to be sold.

Can you name these tropical fruits?

19

WEIRD AND WONDERFUL FRUIT

The lychee comes from southern China and is high in vitamin C.

The rambutan comes from Southeast Asia and is sweet and juicy. Many people in this area grow rambutans in their gardens.

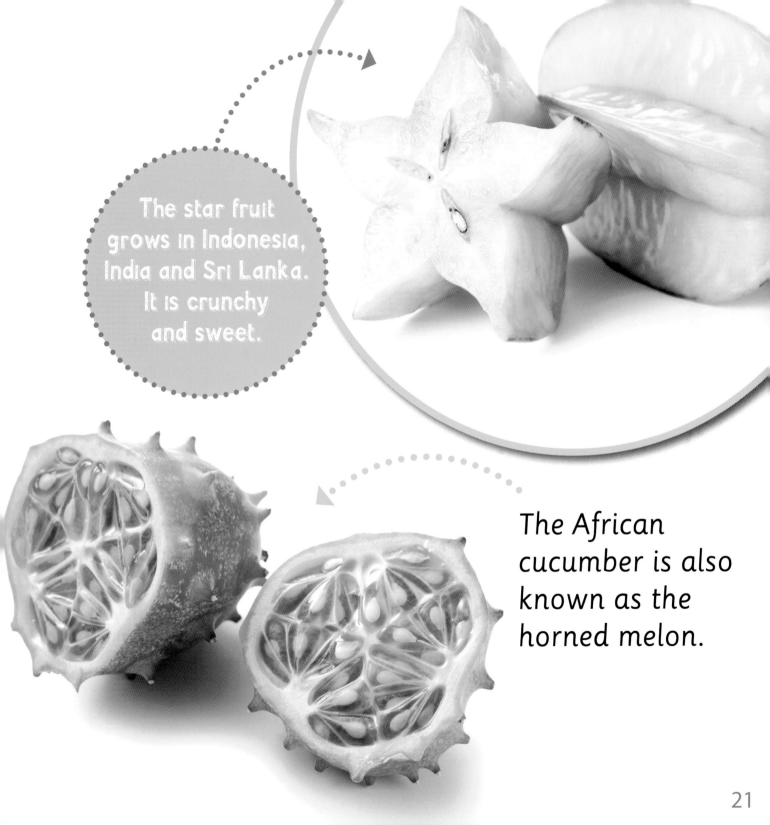

The star fruit grows in Indonesia, India and Sri Lanka. It is crunchy and sweet.

The African cucumber is also known as the horned melon.

FOODY FACTS

Square melons are grown by Japanese farmers for easy storage.

A strawberry isn't actually a berry, but a banana is.

There is a tree called the fruit salad tree that can grow up to 7 different types of fruit.

The world's most popular fruit is the tomato.

GLOSSARY

allotments
land used for growing fruit and vegetables

climates
the common weather in certain areas

raw
not cooked

ripe
ready to be eaten

vitamins and minerals
substances in our bodies that keep us healthy

INDEX

PHOTO CREDITS

Photocredits: Abbreviations: l-left, r-right, b-bottom, t-top, c-centre, m-middle.

Front Cover, 3br, 8inset — Valentina Razumova. 2 — leonori. 3tr,16 — vesna cvorovic. 4bl — Jan Martin Will. 4inset — Tim UR. 5bc — Maks Narodenko. 5tr — Beata Becla. 6 — Sergey Ryzhov. 7bl — Picsfive. 7tr — Johannes Kornelius. 8 — Nitr. 9inset — ISchmidt. 9 — FWStudio. 10bl, 10mr — arka38. 10tl — NinaM. 10tr — Madlen. 10inset — Kelly Marken. 11 — Mila Atkovska. 12 — Tom Wang. 13 — EM Arts. 13inset — Everything. 14 — Peter Zijlstra. 14inset — Adisa. 15 — Kenishirotie. 17bc — Nestor Bandrivskyy. 17inset — zcw. 18l — OlgaLis. 18inset — Alena Haurylik. 19 — Valentyn Volkov. 20tr — Anna Kucherova. 20bl — 9comeback. 21tr — Anna Sedneva. 21bl — Jiri Hera. 22bl — Anna Kucherova. 22tr — Orkhan Aslanov. 23br — Pressmaster. 23tl — Varts. Images are courtesy of Shutterstock.com. With thanks to Getty Images, Thinkstock Photo and iStockphoto. Thank you to Denise Bentulan for use of her typeface Moonflower http://douxiegirl.com/fonts.